LEVEL 2 READER

Forest Babies

by
Joan Emerson

Scholastic Inc.

PHOTO CREDITS:

Photos ©: cover: rpbirdman/iStockphoto; back cover: Rolf Kopfle/Alamy Images; 1: rpbirdman/iStockphoto; 2 leaves and throughout: Textures.com; 2 wood texture background and throughout: t_kimura/iStockphoto; 3: Steve Byland/Dreamstime; 3 sticks and throughout: nopow/iStockphoto; 4 other tree cones and throughout: Knaupe/iStockphoto; 4 pine cone and throughout: Floortje/iStockphoto; 5: Rolf Kopfle/Alamy Images; 6: rpbirdman/iStockphoto; 9: S.J. Krasemann/Getty Images; 10: Adam Lyon; 13: Michelle Gilders/Alamy Images; 14: Erich Kuchling/Getty Images; 17: geoffkuchera/Fotolia; 18: Top-Pics TBK/Alamy Images; 21: Jason Ondreicka/ Dreamstime; 22: Terry Whittaker/FLPA/Minden Pictures; 25: Fuse/Getty Images; 26: F. Lukasseck/Masterfile; 29: Janusz Pie kowski/123RF; 30: David Glassey/Alamy Images.

ISBN 978-1-338-16999-7

The publisher does not have any control over and does not assume any responsibility for author or third-party websites or their content.

10 9 8 7 6 5 4 3 2 1   17 18 19 20 21

Printed in China   68

First printing, September 2017

Produced by Scholastic Inc., 557 Broadway, New York, NY 10012
Scholastic UK Ltd., Euston House, 24 Eversholt Street, London NW1 1DB

Book design by Marissa Asuncion
Photo research by Cynthia Carris

INTRODUCTION

Forests are large wooded areas full of trees and shrubs. They can be found in countries all over the world. Many baby animals make their homes in forests. Some of them live in the tall trees, some live in the wet soil, and some live underground. Turn the page to meet some of the world's cutest forest babies!

AMERICAN RED SQUIRREL

American red squirrels are found in forests throughout North America. They **hibernate** and store food just like common gray squirrels. But their fur is red instead! They are also much smaller than common forest squirrels. And the babies, called kits, are even smaller. When a kit is born, it only weighs a little more than a quarter!

Many **generations** of red squirrel families store their food in the same place.

AMERICAN BLACK BEAR

Black bears are the most common bears in North America. These bears can weigh over 500 pounds. They are also excellent tree climbers. Even though they are called black bears, these animals can be brown, blue-gray, or even white. Black bears hibernate in the winter, but a mother bear can wake up to give birth and care for her cubs. When it is born, a black bear cub weighs less than one pound.

Most black bears are born in litters of two to three cubs.

WHITE-TAILED DEER

The white-tailed deer is the smallest type of deer in North America. A baby deer, called a fawn, has small white spots that cover its fur. The spots **camouflage** the fawn and help keep it safe from **predators**. As the deer gets older, it grows a full brown coat. At birth, fawns weigh less than an average house cat. But white-tailed deer can grow up to 300 pounds when they are adults.

A white-tailed deer can jump up to 10 feet high and run up to 30 miles per hour!

AMERICAN PINE MARTEN

The pine marten is found in Alaska, Canada, and the northern United States. It is about the length of a house cat—but it weighs much less! Because of its small size, the marten can climb trees and jump from treetop to treetop. If it falls, the marten can twist its body in the air so it lands on its paws—from as high as 60 feet in the air!

An American pine marten's tail is about one third the length of its entire body.

NEW WORLD PORCUPINE

The New World porcupine is the biggest kind of porcupine. It can be found in North American forests. A porcupine is a rodent that has more than 30,000 sharp, needle-like **quills**. The quills lie flat most of the time. When a porcupine is threatened, its quills stick up to prick predators. A baby porcupine is called a porcupette. Its quills are soft at birth. But in just a few days the quills harden so it can protect itself.

A newborn porcupine weighs less than a pound.

RED FOX

Red foxes make homes all over the world. They can be found in Europe, Asia, America, and Africa. In North America, red foxes usually live in forests and build **dens** underground. Red fox babies can be called kits, pups, or cubs. At birth, a red fox can weigh about the same as an apple and has brown or gray fur. Its fur turns reddish-brown as the fox grows older. Every winter, a red fox's fur grows thicker to keep it warm.

A red fox's den has a series of tunnels connecting smaller rooms.

BOBCAT

Bobcats are the most common wildcat in North America. There are about one million of them in the United States. These cats are not often seen because they are sneaky **nocturnal** animals. Bobcats are known for their short, or "bobbed," tails. As a kitten, a bobcat weighs less than a pound. As an adult, it grows to be twice as big as an average house cat.

A bobcat can pounce on its **prey** from over 10 feet away!

TIMBER WOLF

Timber wolves, also known as gray wolves, are the largest of all **canines**. Timber wolves are pack animals, which means they live together. Sometimes a pack has up to twenty wolves. All of the wolves help care for a litter of pups. A wolf pup weighs a little more than a can of soda at birth. Soon, a baby timber wolf joins its pack, where it runs, tumbles, and even plays hide-and-seek with the other pups.

Wolves use their barks, whimpers, and howls to talk to other pack members.

GRAY TREEFROG

The gray treefrog is a common frog that lives in treetops across the United States and Canada. Despite its name, this treefrog is not always gray. It can also be green or brown in color to help it blend into its surroundings. The newborn frogs, called tadpoles, hatch from eggs laid in water. They weigh about one ounce. After six to eight weeks, they become small frogs.

A gray treefrog can freeze about 80% of its body to survive cold winters.

WOODLAND VOLE

The woodland vole is a mouselike rodent that lives in forests in the eastern and midwestern United States. Voles live most of their lives in underground burrows with their family. Voles are small animals. At birth, the pups weigh about as much as a penny. As adults, voles only weigh about as much as a slice of bread. Voles are known as pests because they sometimes eat the bulbs people plant in their gardens.

Voles usually only live about three months.

COYOTE

Coyotes live all over America in forests and mountains. But they have **adapted** to live in big cities, too. Coyotes will eat anything. They hunt animals like rabbits, fish, and **rodents**, and they also eat fruits and grass. In the winter, coyotes live and hunt in packs. Baby coyotes, called pups, become a member of the pack as soon as they are born. A newborn coyote weighs only as much as a can of soup!

Coyotes can run up to 40 miles per hour!

MOUNTAIN LION

Mountain lions live all over North and South America—from forests in Canada to the fields of Argentina. These big cats can also be called pumas or cougars. They are the largest wildcats in North America. Mountain lions are excellent hunters. They prey on porcupines, coyotes, and even deer. The baby cubs are born blind and deaf and weigh about the same as a football. But within a couple of months, they learn how to run, jump, and stalk their prey.

Mountain lions can leap onto a tree 15 feet high!

MOOSE

Moose are the largest members of the deer family. These animals are found in North America and Europe. Male moose are called bulls. Their giant antlers can grow up to six feet wide! However, each winter, they shed their antlers and new ones grow in their place. A mother moose, called a cow, gives birth to one baby calf at a time. The calf weighs about the same as a preschooler when it is born!

Moose are great swimmers—they can swim up to six miles per hour!

HEDGEHOG

Hedgehogs are **mammals** that can live in a variety of **habitats**, including forests. Hedgehogs are commonly found in Europe, Africa, and Asia. Hedgehogs have spines that look a lot like a porcupine's quills. When a hedgehog is threatened, it rolls into a very tight ball with its sharp spines facing outward. At birth, a hedgehog baby, or hoglet, is a little smaller than a playing card. Its soft spines appear within a day or so of being born. They become harder after a few weeks.

Hedgehogs can survive many kinds of snake venom.

GLOSSARY

adapt: to change to fit a different situation

camouflage: natural coloring that allows an animal to hide by looking like its surroundings

canine: of or having to do with dogs

den: the home of a wild animal

generation: the direct family members from a shared ancestor

habitat: the place where an animal or plant is usually found

hibernate: to sleep for the entire winter

litter: a number of baby animals that are born at the same time to the same mother

mammal: a warm-blooded animal that has hair or fur and usually gives birth to live babies

nocturnal: active at night

predator: an animal that hunts other animals for food

prey: an animal that is hunted by another animal for food

quill: hollow, sharp spine

rodent: a mammal with large, sharp front teeth that are constantly growing and used for gnawing